THEN AND NOW SERIES: No. 1

Plymouth:
The Reconstruction
of a Blitzed City

Sydney V. C. Goodman

BASKET STREET AND BEDFORD STREET
The gaunt shell of Plymouth's Guildhall is still open to the skies a year or so after the blitz with almost all the nearby buildings in much the same state.

This version of the book is virtually as originally published, presenting the work of Sydney VC Goodman. There are now additional pages at the back providing information about the publisher, Arthur L Clamp.

The republishing project is being managed by Arthur's grandson, Steven Gibson. We aim to find all the research that he was involved in publishing, preserving it for the next generation as part of 'The Clamp Collection'.

INTRODUCTION

As a garrison city Plymouth expected to become involved in the war with Germany. This year, 1985, we celebrate the fact that there has been peace in Europe for forty years, an uneasy peace, but peace.

The devastation of the city began on Saturday, 6th July, 1940, when the first of the many air raids took place. These reduced the city centre to rubble and inflicted high casualities amongst the civilian population. Many well-known buildings and landmarks disappeared, landmarks that were the meeting places of generations of Plymothians never to be replaced as the planning for re-construction got underway. The defences of Plymouth had been strengthened by warships and land forces but still the enemy bombers came unloading their cargoes of death and destruction. Not only Plymouth but Stonehouse and Devonport were badly damaged. Today Plymouth has been rebuilt; Stonehouse and Devonport have not fared as well as may be seen at the western end of Union Street and Marlborough Street. Throughout these raids the civilian population went about their daily chores from cooking in a biscuit tin under a fire, to walking to work amidst the rubble often detouring because of an unexploded bomb. Memories of these times still linger in the mind be they good or bad; the variety of meals made from dried egg powder and the meagre ration of tea or meat. I still remember and like corned beef pasty.

As the war in Europe dragged on Plymouth had its last air raids in April, 1944. During these the Western National bus depot at Prince Rock was burnt out with many buses lost or damaged. Whilst we live and hope that future generations never undergo this experience, the civilian population that was left in the city helped each other in many ways; they were injured but not beaten. After the war had ended children, like myself who had been evacuated, returned to the city to find many of their old schools had been bombed and they had to fit into whatever others could take them.

As the planning went ahead for the re-building programmes the citizens of Plymouth were kept informed of what was to come through the *Western Morning News* and *Western Evening Herald* with photographs and detailed drawings. Open planning resulted in many familiar streets disappearing as clearing up operations began. Bedford Street, Frankfort Street, Russell Street, Basket Street and many more were to be replaced by Royal Parade, Armada Way, Western Approach and Mayflower Street. New buildings were to be erected, the first being that of E. Dingle and Co. in Royal Parade.

During the planning and reconstrtuction it was said at the time that it would cater to the needs of Plymothians for many generations. Does it? The increase in traffic, lack of entertainment, sporting facilities, to name a few. Were the planners foresighted enough to meet these needs? Older generations of Plymothians remember the ice rank, corn exchange, Ballards and other popular places of entertainment and also reflect on the many beautiful buildings that were demolished to make way for the new Plymouth.

In this publication I have used photographs of old Plymouth, damaged by wartime bombing and the new city, these being taken roughly in line with the older photographs though some may be a little off line due to new buildings being in the way. From the old city only a few landmarks remain. Other well-known places such as *Harvest Home*, Millbay Station, Ballards, Corn Exchange and Prudential building have since disappeared. Union Street was once known the world over through men of the Royal Navy. Would they recognise it today? As a boy I well remember the times I cycled to Drakes Circus only to come off my bicycle on the tarred blocks on a rainy day and to return home with torn trousers and bleeding knees. Tin Pan Alley and the Pannier Market. Compare today's Woolworth stores in New George Street with their stalls in the market or today's supermarket with Maypoles in Ebrington Street where butter and margarine were weighed out with butter pats. The smell of the various provisions would waft out the door to meet you. Compare that with today's pre-packaging. The Palace Theatre where you sat in the Gods then, on the way home, went to Dewdneys in King Street for a pasty or Taylors for pig's feet!

It is very rare today to re-capture that atmosphere. In those early post-war days we could watch the passengers alight from the Star buses in East Street as they made their way to the market or shops that were open. Heybrook Bay and Wembury conjured up the idea they were miles from Plymouth! As time went by rail excursions went to seaside resorts that were re-opening. A day trip to Goodrington was talked of for days. Visitors to the city are often quoted as saying, "What a beautiful city you have and modern shops." Do we appreciate what we have or is it taken for granted? Are we enjoying life as did the pre-war Plymothians or has television, videos and discos become the order of the day and family life gone by the board?

Sporting facilities have improved but no longer do we have speedway, dog racing, pony racing and many other outdoor sports. Are we getting what we would like or have the city fathers, over the years, pressed on us what they wanted? Christmas lights were once an attractive feature when shopping trips to Plymouth were organised from country communities. Have the traders in Plymouth decided that they only want our custom, some have seen fit not to contribute towards the finance of this scheme. Organisations in Plymouth do their best but more could be achieved. Are we as Plymothians better off with a new city or were pre-war Plymothians with low wages and inferior housing more content with life?

I would like to thank the *Western Evening Herald* for the use of many photographs and Dave Crispin who had the task of taking the new photographs to link the old with the new. I would also like to remember my late father, Charles Goodman, for many photographs he collected during his life as a bus driver with Plymouth City Transport.

S.V.C. Goodman.

Looking towards the Hoe

Barclays Bank building was one of the first to be built in this vicinity. Cars are passing along the line of the future Armada Way and the wartime huts and nearby building stood for only a few more years. The scene below as viewed in 1985 from the tower of the Guildhall showing the former Law Courts in the foreground.

St. Andrew's Cross

The contrast between these views could not be greater with both showing the spire of Charles Church in their background. The christmas tree stands alone in the middle of the roundabout and the rubble of the blitz has been cleared in preparation for new buildings.

Old Town Street

Looking down this once familiar street at a time when the new kerbstones were being laid and the alignment of what was to be New George Street determined. Now the area is crowded with shoppers and part of the street made into a pedestrian area.

Westwell Street

Westwell Street before the war with deliveries being made by a brewer's dray to the *Town Hall Vaults* Hotel. Tram car No. 11 is on service No. 4 to Beaumont Road. The results of enemy bombing on the building with the tower of the Guildhall still unscathed.

The Guildhall Tower

Like a sentinel the tower stands well above more damage inflicted around it. The trams are not running but the overhead wires are still in position. The tower today with open spaces, trees and flower beds covering the area with Dingles store in the background.

ST. ANDREW'S CROSS

The crowded pre-war scene just outside St. Andrew's Church eventually gave way to the tree-lined Royal Parade with little remaining apart from the church and ornamented stone pillars.

Old Frankfort Street—New George Street

The only building in both photographs is the Leicester Harmsworth House, home of the *Western Morning News*. Built in the late 1930s it withstood the fires of the raids and now forms part of the frontage of New George Street.

Old Market and Corn Exchange

Some buildings survived the many bombing raids and these here along East Street will bring back memories as will the view below with shoppers buying their daily needs from what was called *Tin Pan Alley*. Now Cornwall Street covers this area.

The New Market

These two views show the modern market at the bottom of Cornwall Street which replaced the old buildings. Although not welcomed at first, the modern market is always full of people and stallholders have a busy time meeting requests for a thousand and one items.

Charles Church

The bombed Charles Church stands well above the cleared blitzed areas and stands as a memorial to the citizens who lost their lives in the raids. The new viaduct is in position and, in the lower photograph, the car park and garage make up part of the scene as it is today.

LOOKING WEST ALONG UNION STREET

The railway bridge which used to carry trains to Millbay remained for many years after the war but many buildings in the upper scene made way for a wider road and newer buildings as recorded below.

Looking up Royal Parade

The Royal Parade was officially opened in 1947 and here, a little later, old and new buildings bridge the changes then taking place in the heart of Plymouth. Today's view of the same area shows the completed scheme of rebuilding.

Looking down Royal Parade

This is now in use and the steel structures of at least two buildings are in position. The lower picture shows the completed frontage of the now well-known departmental stores and shops facing the Royal Parade.

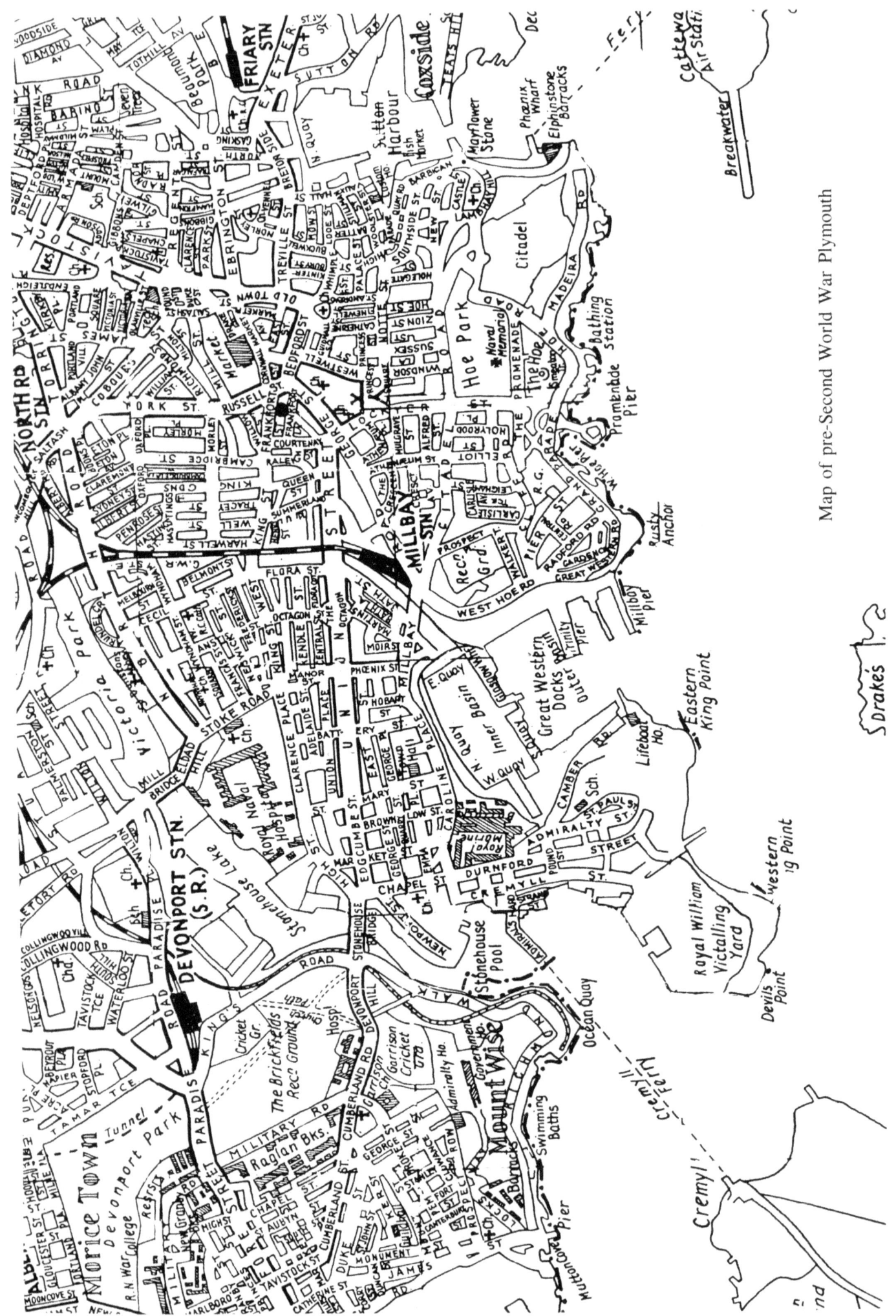

Map of pre-Second World War Plymouth

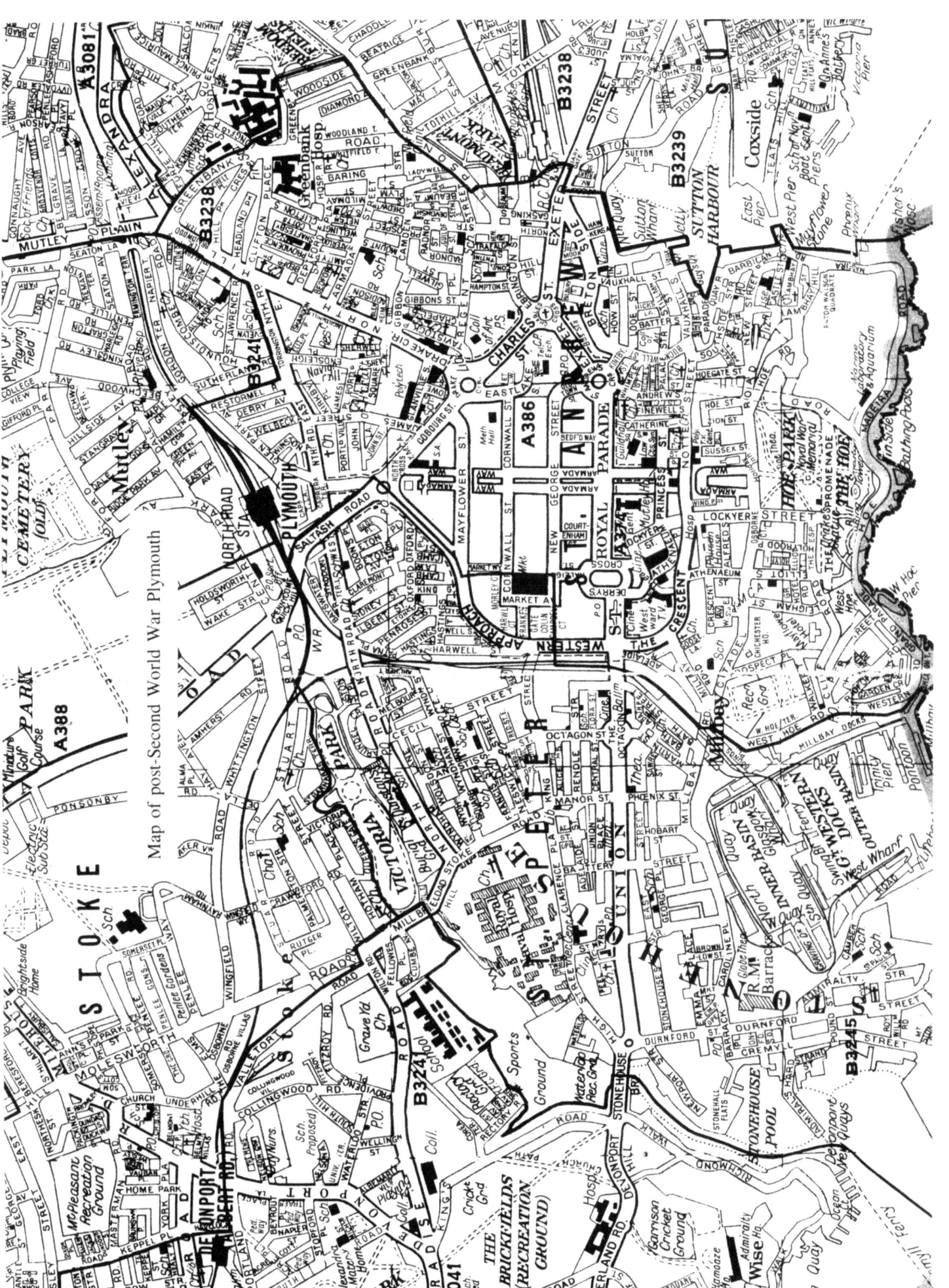

Map of post-Second World War Plymouth

Derry's Clock

This early picture, taken from the old Theatre Royal looking east towards George Street, shows the tramlines and horse-drawn bus beyond the clock. The contemporary view includes part of the new Theatre Royal.

Notte Street

Partial damage to the buildings is recorded here although more was to come in later raids. The wide street is now fronted with large banks and offices and carries much traffic through the city.

Looking North from Drake's Drum Flagstaff

A very neat and almost traffic-free new Royal Parade is viewed against the old Prudential building and cleared areas of the blitzed centre of the city. The flagstaff was later moved to its present position seen below with part of the Pearl Assurance building forming one side to the Armada Way.

Royal Parade

This scene, taken after 1947, shows various buildings that survived the numerous bombing including the Co-operative store, on the left, and the Odeon cinema behind it. These and all the others have made way for much larger stores as seen below.

Union Street

Looking east along Union Street towards Derry's Clock before the blitz with a tram on its way to Devonport. The scene today with the civic centre in the background and some properties still in position along the right hand side of the street.

North Cross Roundabout

Clearance work begins for the new roads and roundabout along Cobourg Street just above North Road railway station. The houses on the right are still standing but today's picture of the area shows it now almost occupied by a large roundabout and pedestrian thoroughfare.

Exeter Street

This part of the city was not so heavily damaged as the main shopping area. The changes have come from the planners who widened the old street and built the present main dual carriageway. This is under construction at the top and completed below both showing Charles Church in the background.

North Road Railway Station

The station as it was built is in the upper photograph although Park Avenue has not yet been built. Areas of Mutley can be seen in the background. The new station building, now known as *Plymouth Station*, replaced the old in the 1960s and became the principal station in the city following the demise of Millbay and Friary station.

Raleigh Street

The start of the development of post-war Plymouth is captured in the upper view with many old buildings awaiting the bulldozer to enable modern buildings to take their place as seen below viewed from the middle of the large roundabout.

New George Street

This is being laid down and diverges from the former Frankfort Street seen beyond the newspaper offices. The *Prince of Wales* Hotel has little time left to be replaced by the buildings viewed in the lower view taken from Dingles large store.

Drakes Circus

Another well known landmark to survive the blitz but not the planners was the large office block with familiar clock and letters. The area has been radically changed as recorded by this contemporary photograph below.

Drake's Drum Flagstaff

This marks the rebuilding programme for Plymouth and was unveiled in 1947. The civic building stands where the nisson huts are and a pedestrian underway runs down from the flagstaff. The area is shown below as it is in 1985.

Royal Parade

The construction of Plymouth's main thoroughfare is well under way and many buildings still standing from the blitz were to come down to make way for the new centre of the city. The Theatre Royal now dominates the west end and faces the many large post-ware stores.

Technical College and Tavistock Road

Tavistock Road looking north with the old Technical College building known to many Plymouth students. This view is from the long gone *Harvest Home*. Part of the large Polytechnic building overlooks the road which has been considerably widened.

Armada Way

Christmas decorations enhance this post-war thoroughfare running from near the Hoe to North Cross roundabout. Part of it is constructed in the upper photograph and its alignment can be identified by E. Dingle's new store on the left side of this scene.

Arthur L. Clamp – the man behind the books

Arthur Leslie Clamp was a man of boundless energy with a passion for helping others, particularly through his love of history. A printer by trade, he started his career in a printing company before moving his family from Exeter to Plymouth to teach at the Plymouth College of Art and Design, where he eventually became the Head of the Printing Department.

Arthur with his five children.

A Devoted Family Man

Despite his love of teaching, Arthur prioritised his family, always making it home by 5:30pm for tea. He and his wife, Rosemary, raised five children: Susan, Angela, Elizabeth, David, and Steven. Arthur would often combine his love of family and history by taking his children on Sunday walks, encouraging them to appreciate historical monuments by taking photos or making crayon rubbings of gravestones for his books. The family home at 203 Elburton Road was a hub of activity, with a large garden, featuring a two-storey fort and a makeshift swimming pool.

A Lifelong Learner and Adventurer

Arthur's thirst for knowledge extended beyond history to a deep curiosity about the world. He was passionate about exploring different cultures, traditions, and cuisines, often taking advantage of his long summer holidays as a teacher to travel to places like India, Russia, South America, the middle east and the USA, sometimes bringing one of his children along. This adventurous spirit even influenced his home life, as seen by the short-lived family tradition of steam-cooking vegetables after a trip to Iceland.

History is a prominent feature of family days out

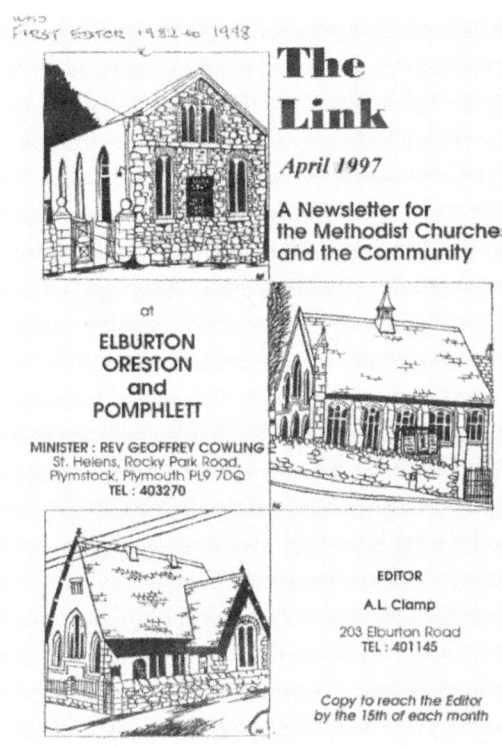

Community and Philanthropic Spirit

His commitment to serving others was evident in his long-standing involvement with the Elburton Methodist Church. He was the Sunday School Superintendent for over 15 years and served as the editor of the wider church's monthly newsletter, "The Link," for a similar duration. After Rosemary's very sad passing, Arthur later remarried and, following a chance encounter with a professor from India, established a connection with a missionary school in Chennai. Together with his new wife, Christine, he co-founded a "Sponsor a Child's Education" program that continues to this day.

*Pictured left – The cover of 'The Link' complete
with hand drawn sketches of each church by Angela
Below right – Arthur Clamp promoting his latest book
Below left – Arthur at home with his first wife, Rosemary
Below centre – Arthur on holiday with his second wife,
Christine*

A Legacy of Learning and Positivity

Arthur's greatest passion was history, which he brought to life through tireless research, documentation, and the many books he authored. He was driven by a need to "never be stuck in a rut," constantly seeking new experiences, meeting new people, and expanding his knowledge. With a positive attitude and a great sense of humour, he was always ready to help others, leaving a lasting impact on his family and community. His children, Susan, Angela, Elizabeth, David, and Steven, remember him with love and gratitude.

David Clamp, 2025

A Legacy of Local History

Below is the story of how Arthur L Clamp began writing books, in his own words, drafted shortly before he passed away in 2001. I have only made minor alterations to this text, correcting grammatical errors that he did not survive to correct himself. When I first discovered this text, I was shocked to see my name mentioned. It seems that, unbeknownst to me, I shared my first PC with him. I suspect he used it during the day when I was at school, although I do have one memory of sitting with him and showing him how it worked. It has been a pleasure to pick up where he left off and see his books republished and redistributed, and to know that I was part of the story, even back then. It was also fascinating to discover that his pricing structure matches the way I have tried to price the books, with a third going to local sellers and the rest covering printing costs with a little left over for my expenses.

I am his eldest grandson, and it is a privilege to curate his legacy, which we are calling 'The Clamp Collection'. The very last line of the text originally reads "The following pages list all the titles." Sadly, that page is missing and we have no record of all the books he published and knowing that some of those were researched by other authors makes the process of finding them even harder. I look forward to one day completing the collection and seeing them all available again. And maybe, one day, I'll even start writing my own to add to the series. For now, here is his story in his own words.

Steven Gibson, 2025

Writing and Publishing Booklets on Local Topics and Areas

I started this interest in either 1968 or 1969 when living in Woodford. I had by these dates established the Department of Printing and I think I must have been looking for something different to do. The first titles were of A5 size proofed from type set at Clarke, Doble and Brendon, Ltd., Plymouth printers, and then made up into pages and printed at Sawtell and Neilson, Ltd., Totnes.

Then began a slow process of getting them out to shops, etc. which proved to be more time consuming and difficult than actually researching, writing and getting the books into print. However, I persisted and opened a business account with Barclays Bank on the Broadway. I was advised to give it a title so I called it "Westway Publications". There came along another problem, one of storage of paper and finished books which was solved when the family moved to Elburton in 1970.

I changed the printer to Penwell, Ltd., Callington, Cornwall, as he was then just setting up himself and his prices seemed very reasonable. I did not get any of the printers to make up the complete books. I hand folded the flat printed sheets, stitched the books on a small manual table stitcher and trimmed them in a small hand turned guillotine which I bought from someone in Penzance for £40. It was brought up in a van.

The trouble and time going to and fro to Callington was too much so I transferred the printing to PDS Printers, Prince Rock, Plymouth, and I have been with them ever since. Now they are at Plympton which is easy to reach and they fold the flat sheets which was turning out to be a long chore which only saved a small part of the printing costs.

All my first titles were written by myself. I took the photographs and developed them in the loft of the house, the type was set by now on a computer situated in the house at Elburton from which I had collected photographic lengths of text to cut up and law down as pages.

At some point I decided that I would do my own film processing of lith film so I bought a large second hand process camera from Kingsbridge and learnt through trial and error to make line negatives of the text and halftone negatives of the illustrations which proved more difficult than I anticipated. The main problem was trying to keep the developer in the large dish at the correct temperature as any change would affect the developing time. I replaced this old camera with a brand new one bought from Croydon, Surrey, costing £900. This has turned out to be a great asset cutting out an expensive part of the printer's costs and one crucial aspect of the work which I could control.

By the middle 1970s there were many outlets I had contacted in Plymouth, up to Dartmoor, Exeter, around to Torbay, Totnes, Dartmouth and the South Hams. The market for local books was much greater than I had first thought and through getting to know many local people undertaking research themselves had the chance to help and make up books for other people who had in most instances, got together a collection of photographs with some text in a rather muddled way. Through my experience in print I was able to shape up their work and get it into print and in every case I had to pay the printer and let the person have the royalties. In the majority of titles produced in this manner this was another way of producing titles and it did give some profit to my work. However, I must say that in a few cases I lost out by either the other person getting the numbers wrong, not returning any monies from stock I delivered or they thought that more of their books should have been sold.

The print run was usually 1,000 copies and from time to time I have had reprints of 250 copies. It took about ten years to clear the first print run so I always had large stocks in the garage, workshop, etc. The numbers sold during the early years was about 7,000 copies a year increasing to around 9,000 copies and for the whole of the enterprise about 500,000 have been sold. The booklets have become part of the local scene and many people collect them, shops regularly order copies and I go around certain areas month by month restocking or replacing titles as necessary.

During the past year or so I have started setting the text on a Packard Bell PC, something which I should have done some years back. I share it with Steven Gibson, my grandson. There appears to be no end to the market for local books, but I could not earn a regular income because of the long time it takes to sell stock.

However, now exceeding 100 titles made up mainly of A4 twenty-four page booklets, some folded guides, with selling prices set with a third going to the shop which is the trade custom, the original idea has been quite successful and could go on for ever.

Apart from monetary benefits, however spasmodically these might be, I have learnt a lot myself, met many interesting people and have become part of the local scene with requests to give talks and to advise people about getting into print.

Arthur L Clamp, 2001

This newspaper article, published by the Evening Herald on 17th August 2001, forms a good record of his life. Just as he encourages us to learn more about local history, we encourage you to learn a little about him. For that reason, we have included these pages at the back of all the most recently republished books, in honour of his memory and recognition of his contribution to the community.

www.ingramcontent.com/pod-product-compliance
Lightning Source LLC
Chambersburg PA
CBHW061404070526
44584CB00031B/4162